Presented to

_____

from

_____

on

_____

MOMENTS WITH GOD

Text by
MARY PAOLINI

Photographs by
HANK MORGAN

Foreword by Louis M. Savary

THE REGINA PRESS   •   New York

1975
THE REGINA PRESS
7 Midland Avenue
Hicksville, New York 11801

Library of Congress Catalog Card Number: 75-15413
ISBN 0-88271-028-1

Manufactured in the United States of America

Foreword

Moments with God should prove invaluable in helping your children begin a genuine sharing-relationship with God.

When children find a toy that was lost, or jump with excitement at a party, or learn to do a new task by themselves, they need to share such special moments with others. They hasten to tell a parent, a brother, sister, friend—or any person to whom they feel close.

Moments with God suggests how experiences like these may also be shared with God. Such sharing helps form loving bonds between the child and God.

Louis M. Savary

SPECIAL MOMENTS

Thank you, dear God, for each new day.
You are with me always
every single moment of every day.
You always think of me.
Sometimes I think of you
and other times I don't.
Sometimes I kneel down and talk to you
and other times I just know you're there.
Do you know why, God?
Because there are special moments
when you come close to me
when I feel safe, happy, excited—
even times when I feel sad, lonely or scared.
And I lift my heart and mind to you.
These are my moments with you.
I can share them with you.
You are with me now.
Today.

YOU ARE ALWAYS LISTENING

Do you know, dear God,
who my very favorite person
in this whole, wide world is?
It's you.
Because I can tell you secrets.
I can tell you how I really feel
when I'm sad,
or mad,
or when I've been a little bit bad.
I can talk to you.
You are our Father in heaven.
Sometimes grownups
don't have time to listen.
I know they're busy.
That's why I'm glad
I have you.
You are always here
listening to me, dear Father.

IT'S ME, GOD

Do you know
all the things
I can do
with my voice, dear God?
I can sing,
I can cry,
I can shout,
I can whisper,
I can laugh
and I can say,
"Let's play"
or "Wow!"
or "I like you"
and then people know I'm around.

But I don't have to talk out loud to you, Father.
I can talk to you inside my head.
You always know me.

9

SPEAKING

I can count now, dear Father,
and I know all the numbers.
My mother lets me use the telephone.
Sometimes I can call a friend
all by myself.
I said "Hello."
"Can you come over?"

But I can talk to you anytime, God.
And I don't need a telephone.

LOVE LIKE A CIRCLE

Some things are square
and some things are like circles.
Some have holes inside.
Look, God, I can peek through
and see the world
in a circle.

Your love goes
all around the world
like a circle.

ARE YOU PROUD OF ME, GOD?

Before I couldn't tie my shoes
because I was too little.
You made me grow
taller and smarter.
I can figure out how to tie a bow
all by myself.
Are you proud of me, God?
I'm proud of myself.
I think you must be proud
when I learn
to do hard things—
even if I make mistakes trying.

NEW LIFE

We're making Easter baskets
with colored ribbons.
What color shall I choose?
When this one is finished
we're going to make
another Easter basket.

At Easter we celebrate
the new life you gave
your son, Jesus.
He rose from the dead.
Now we share his new life.

GIVING

When we came out of Church,
I put some money
into the Poor Box.
It's to help poor people.
It's a present from me
to someone I don't even know.
I like to give presents.
It makes me feel good.

You gave us everything, dear Father.
I like to give things, too.

YOU ARE WITH ME

I like being at the park.
I can play
on the swings
and the sliding boards.
I meet my friends there.
We run and make noise.
Sometimes we play hide-and-seek.
Can you see me, God,
When I hide?

Did you see me climb up
a sliding board
and slide all the way down
by myself?
I got scared
the first time
but not anymore.
Now I like to go down sliding boards.

Dear Father, you are with me
in everything I do.

CARING

How powerful and wise you are, God.
You made the swans and ducks
and all the other birds and animals
in the whole, wide world.

I like to come to the pond
and feed bread to the ducks.
They are like pets.
See how they trust us.
I wonder if they're really hungry,
or whether they just like attention.

I think they like attention
just like I do.

I trust you, God.
You are always caring for me.

BEING HAPPY

Look, dear God, who I found
peeking out at us.
I wonder what his name is?
He's wondering about me, too.
He is bigger and stronger than me
but I can tell he's shy.
I won't frighten him
(if he won't frighten me).
I'll talk to him
and make him happy.

You want him to be happy, Father,
just like you want me to be happy.

KNOWING YOU

Look at that, dear God!
Wow!
How does it work?
You know how an engine works
because you know all things.

You gave me a wonderful brain.
I can figure out what makes things work.
Thank you, dear Father,
you made me to be like you—
I can know many things, too.
And I can know you.

GOD IS EVERYWHERE

Do you know what I wish
I could do, God?
I wish I could swim under water
like a fish.
If I had fins
and a swishy tail
I could swim
up and down
and all around
in my big, quiet, cool tank.

Or maybe I would live
in the deep ocean, instead.
You would be there with me, God,
because you are everywhere.

THANK YOU, GOD

Today I found someone
just like me.
I stood in front of her
and everything I did
she did, too.
She even made a funny face
when I did.
When I'd reach out
to touch her
she'd reach out to touch me!
When I peeked at her,
she did the same
right back at me.
Whatever I did
she did, too.
We had fun.

Thank you, dear God,
for making me.

PLAYING BY MYSELF

I went to the beach today
and played by myself
in the warm sand.
Did you ever feel sand
between your toes?
Did you ever let it pour
through your fingers?
Sometimes I build castles and roads.
And sometimes I find buried treasures
like shells.

Thank you, Father,
for making this world
so full of so many places to play.

LOVE FOREVER

I found some grown-up clothes
to wear so I can play "mother."
I put on a pair of shoes.
Listen!
Don't they make a funny noise
when I walk around?

I won't forget about you, God
when I am big and tall and different-looking.
I'll still be me.
And I know you'll love me forever.
I will love you, too.

SECRETS

I have a secret!
I ask my friend to
promise not to tell.
If he won't,
I'll whisper it
in his ear.

God, you have lots of secrets!
Why don't you tell me a few?
When it's quiet
and I'm thinking about you
it seems like you're telling me secrets.

A FRIEND LIKE YOU

I have one friend who is special
because he makes me feel special.
That's the way you make me feel, too, God.

I like to be with him.
He smiles at me.
He listens to me.
He lets me go first.
He doesn't call me names.
He doesn't get mad.
He understands me.

You are like a special friend, dear Father.

HELP ME, GOD

Most of the time
I try very hard
not to make mistakes.
But sometimes I do.
I know you understand
and you'll let me try again.

You want us to keep trying, Father.
That's what matters.
Please help me, OK?

LAUGHING

I like to drink
from a fountain in the park.
Sometimes the water
squirts up high
and gets my face all wet!
Sometimes it just trickles out
and won't shoot up at all.
Then I put my finger
against the water
so I can make it
come up higher and faster!

It feels good to laugh, dear God.

BEING ALIVE

Look! God, can you see me?
Maybe I'm going too fast!
I'm scared, but I'm laughing!
Isn't that funny?

Some rides go way up high
in the sky.
Some go round and round
on the ground.

I like any of them
that go real fast!
It's exciting.

Lots of times I think
just being alive
is exciting.

A HAPPY FEELING DEEP INSIDE

I go up and down
and all around
on the big merry-go-round.
I hold on tight, God.
And the music makes me happy.
I wish I could stay on
for ten rides—or more.
It's like being in a special world
of music and colored lights
and a happy-feeling
that starts deep inside.

You know what I mean, God,
because you made me to be happy.
You want me to be happy with you forever.

A SPECIAL TREAT

We ate homemade ice cream.
Grandfather made it
just for us—a special treat.
We sat outside
eating the ice cream
in big sugar cones.
Mine melted
and some got all over
my hands and face.
I can wipe it off.

Thank you for ice cream, God.
And thank you for making
the people who make ice cream.

A SECRET PLACE

I'm going to a secret place.
No one knows where it is.
Only you know, God.
I climb way up over the rocks.
It's my very own place.
Sometimes I go and sit
and look around.
It makes me feel good
to have a special hide-out.
I know I can go there
whenever I want.

If I want to,
I can think about you
and talk to you.
It's very quiet.

YOU KNOW ME ANYWAY

It's Halloween
and I made a mask
to wear over my head.
Do you think anyone
will recognize me?
Do you think anyone
will be afraid of me?

Is anyone afraid of you, God?
I'm not afraid of you.
I know you know me anyway
and you love me
even when I have a mask on.

I love you, dear God,
even though I can't see you!

THANK YOU FOR SNOW

The snow is all over the ground, God.
Do you see our footprints in it?
We're going to make a snowman.
We'll dress him in my old hat
and give him a big stick.

Our hands get cold
and our noses get red.
When we go in to get warm
mother might give us
hot chocolate and cookies.

Then we'll go out again!
Thank you for snow, God!

CHRISTMAS IS JESUS' BIRTHDAY

I like Christmas, God.
I know it's the birthday
of Jesus, your own son.

I can move the little statues
so the baby Jesus is in the middle
and Mary and Joseph are next to him.
He will be safe and warm and happy.
I put the wise men,
the shepherds
and the animals
all around the baby.
They all want to see him.
He wants to see them, too.

And he can see me.

TELLING GOD ABOUT THINGS I LIKE

Do you know what I like
best of all, God?
Lollipops!
Some people like red ones.
Some like yellow ones.
But I like big ones.

I feel like telling you
about things I like
even if you already know.

YOU KNOW I'M JUST TIRED

Sometimes I get worn out, God.
Sometimes I get mad and cranky
because I'm tired.
You know I don't want to be mean.
You know I just get tired.

If I lie down
and look at some picture books
I begin to feel warm and sleepy.
Then I fall asleep.

Thank you, God, for sleep.

HURTING

I fell down
and cut myself.
I tried not to cry
but it hurt!

Now I have a band-aid
on my knee.
I feel OK.
I don't hurt anymore!

You always understand
how I feel, dear Father.

HOW GREAT YOU ARE

I can look up at the sky
and watch the clouds.
There are all different sizes
and all different shapes—
big, fat clouds,
little wispy clouds.
Some look like animals
and some even look like faces.

The longer I look
the more I can see.

How great the sky is, Father,
and how great you are.

IS THAT YOU, FATHER?

I wonder what I'll be
when I grow up?
I wonder where I'll go?
There are so many things
to do in the world
and places to go.

Sometimes when I go off by myself
and think and wonder,
new ideas come into my head.
Is that you, Father?
Is that one of the ways
you speak to us?
I think so.
I'll listen, OK?

I know you will always be with me, dear God,
whatever I do
and wherever I go.

Here you may write your own prayer to God, in your own words.

Here is My Own Special Prayer